PRAYERS
FOR THE
SERVANTS
OF
GOD

EDWARD HAYS

OTHER BOOKS BY THE AUTHOR:
(available from Forest of Peace Books, Inc.)

In Pursuit of the Great White Rabbit
A Pilgrim's Almanac
Prayers for a Planetary Pilgrim
Prayers for the Domestic Church
Secular Sanctity
Pray All Ways
Twelve and One-Half Keys
The Ethiopian Tattoo Shop
St. George and the Dragon
Sundancer

Forest of Peace Books, Inc.

PRAYERS FOR THE SERVANTS OF GOD
copyright © 1980, by Edward M. Hays

ISBN 0-939516-03-9

published by
Forest of Peace Books, Inc.
Route One - Box 248
Easton, KS 66020   U.S.A.

printed by
Hall Directory, Inc.
Topeka, KS 66608

1st Printing: March 1980
2nd Printing: May 1986
3rd Printing: August 1990

Grateful acknowledgement is given to the following:
Scripture texts used in this work are taken from the NEW AMERICAN BI-BLE, copyright © 1970, by the Confraternity of Christian Doctrine, Washington, D.C., and are used by permission of the copyright owner. All rights reserved.

The verse from Psalm 135 (page 139) is used by permission of The Grail (England).

Dedicated to

Archbishop Ignatius J. Strecker,
Servant of God,
a man of prayer and vision

TABLE OF CONTENTS

INTRODUCTION...........................11

THE SANCTUARY, A SCHOOL FOR SANCTITY....13

Prayer Rituals for a Gathering of Servants
Before and After the Sacred Liturgy..............17
    Common Prayer Ritual of Preparation (1)...............18
    Common Prayer Ritual of Thanksgiving (1)...............19
    Common Prayer of Preparation (2).....................20
    Common Prayer of Thanksgiving (2)....................21

Individual Prayers for Servants
Before and After the Sacred Liturgy..............23
    for a Celebrant......................................24
    for a Deacon or Lay Minister of the Eucharist............26
    for a Lector or Reader of the Word....................28
    for an Acolyte.......................................30
    for a Musician.......................................32
    for an Organist......................................34
    for a Cantor or Choir Member........................36
    for a Servant Involved in Sacred Dance.................38
    for an Usher..40
    for a Servant Counting Money.......................42
    for a Servant Who Prepares the Sanctuary...............44

Prayers for Servants of the Community
Whose Ministry Flows from the Altar.............47
    for a Minister of a Communion Service...................48
    for a Servant Who Takes Communion to the Sick
    or Elderly..50
    for a Servant Who Acts as a Leader of Prayer.............52
    for a Servant Visiting the Sick or Elderly.................54
    for a Servant Visiting the Sick........................56
    for a Director of Religious Education...................58
    for a Teacher of Religion............................60

for a Youth Worker.................................62
for a Servant Bearing Gifts of Aid to Those in Need........64
for a Servant Demonstrating for Social Justice............66
for a Servant Who Works at a Social Event..............68
for a Servant of God (any ministry).....................70
for an Officer on a Parish Council.....................72
for a Member of a Parish Council......................73
for any Elected Officer.............................74

PRACTICE AND PREPARATION AS PRAYER.....76
Prayers for Rehearsal and Preparation...........79
for a Wedding Rehearsal..............................80
for a Wedding Rehearsal..............................82
for the Reception of a Sacrament.....................84
for a Liturgical Function............................86
for a Liturgical Function............................88
for a Music Practice................................89
for a Music Practice................................90
for a Choir Practice................................92
for Preparing a Homily..............................94

THE PRAYER OF THE MEETING...............96
Prayers Before Meetings......................99
before a Parish Council Meeting.......................100
before a Parish Council Meeting.......................101
before a Parish Council Meeting.......................102
before a Parish Council Meeting.......................103
before a Parish Council Meeting.......................104
before an Educational Meeting........................105
before a Liturgy Meeting............................106
before a Liturgy Meeting............................107
before any Meeting.................................108
before any Meeting.................................109
before any Meeting.................................110
at A Time of Stalemate.............................111
Prayers After Meetings......................113
after a Liturgy Meeting............................114
after any Meeting.................................115

after any Meeting.................................116
after any Meeting.................................117
after any Meeting.................................118
after a Long Meeting..............................119
Prayers Before and After a Meeting Using a Sacramental...120

SACRED DRESS FOR THE SERVANTS OF GOD...122
  Prayers of Devotion for the Servants of God.......125
    Prayer of Preparation for One Who Serves..............126
    Prayer for Divine Assistance.........................127
    Prayer for Protection from Routine-Like Ritual
    in the Sacred Liturgy...............................128
    Prayer for Prayerfulness............................129
    Prayer of Gratitude after a Time of Service..............130
    Prayer of Gratitude after a Time of Service..............131
    Prayer of Gratitude after a Time of Service..............132
    Prayer of Gratitude after a Time of Service..............133
    Reflection on the Example of Jesus.....................135
    Reflection on the Reward of Servants...................137
    Mary's Canticle...................................138
    Psalms for Servants...............................139

RENEWAL OF DEDICATION TO SERVICE.......140
    Prayer of Dedication for a Servant of God..............142

INTRODUCTION

In these years of renewal following the Second Vatican Council, we have experienced, through the gift of the Holy Spirit, an explosion of vocations to service within the Christian Community and to the wider world that surrounds it. These opportunities for service are even called "ministries" by some who no longer find it suitable that such a term be reserved for the ordained and established offices of the Church. Regardless of their title, those who are called today to perform works which in times past were performed exclusively by the ordained clergy are indeed serving. Moreover, all who have passed through the mysterious waters of Baptism have been annointed as servants of God and servants of others. And so, those persons who perform such duties as lector, minister of communion or services that flow from the altar, such as visiting the sick, are servants in the image of our Lord, Jesus Christ.

The title "Servant of Yahweh," or "Servant of the Lord" was a distinction among the prophets of Israel commanding great respect. Moses, David, and Elijah, for example, were called servants or slaves of God. Although we who live in a democratic society may find the title of servant to be an uncomfortable one, that very title is applied to Jesus numerous times in the New Testament. As disciples of The Servant of God—Jesus—no title can be for us a greater honor.

Those persons, both ordained and non-ordained, who are called to serve others will hopefully find in that ancient gift of service the royal road to personal growth in holiness. The prayers of this book are simply seeds to bring forth that unfolding spirituality of service, seeds to raise in each servant a consciousness of the Divine Mystery present within every act of service—indeed, within every act.

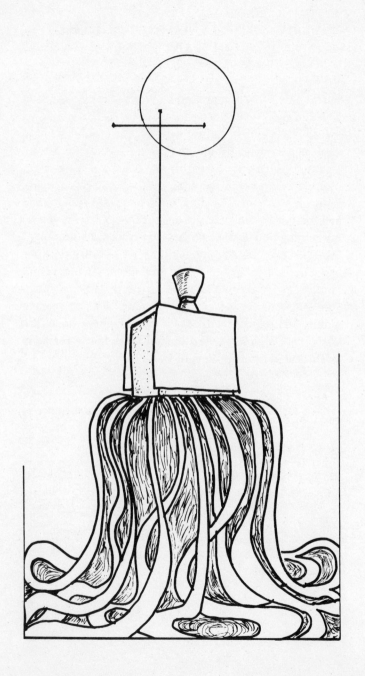

THE SANCTUARY, A SCHOOL
FOR SANCTITY

Surrounding the altar, mysterious sign of the presence of God and table for the sacred meal of the Eucharist, is that sacred circle and school for sanctity, the sanctuary. That circle mysteriously extends to the place of the choir, to the position of the lectors, of the ushers—swelling to wherever servants of the altar and its mysteries are present. Like streams that flow out from that sacred circle and its source, the altar, are such forms of service as taking communion to those unable to be physically present at Mass, the teaching of religious education, care of the poor and elderly, ministry to youth, prayers of healing, visitation of the sick and imprisoned, service through meetings and programs, acts of social service to the parish-community and all other activity that is part of the life of the Christian Community. And each of these holy streams is given flesh by the servants of God.

Those who serve God and the People of God by sacred service are gifted with the pearl of the kingdom, the opportunity to be purified and brought closer to God through the act of selfless service to others. Seen in this light, the act of service contains a genuine ministry of the "served" to the server as well. All, both the served and those who serve, may be called "Servants of God," a title of great honor, acknowledged with pride by the prophets and patriarchs of old. In truth, we have been called by Christ to be His friends, but this friendship is brought to light in the act of washing feet. We are called in the center of this friendship to humble service of each other and the

Church.

In the ancient days, the place of ritual was also the place of instruction and learning. The building was intended to be a classroom where the paintings, stained-glass windows and carvings would be a textbook of scripture and a creed of doctrine. In the spirit of this tradition, I first learned my catechism sitting on a cushioned kneeler in a mission church; my first desk was the seat of a pew. If we understand the meaning of the sacred rites, the church can even today be a school of sanctity for all those who serve there. Each time we celebrate the mysteries of the life and death and resurrection of our Lord, we are being taught the lesson of holiness. Each time we serve others, repeating by deed the humble service of our Lord at His own Last Supper, we find ourselves enrolled in the most ancient, yet most beautiful classroom of the Church.

The Finger of God, as the Holy Spirit is called in the sacred liturgy, traces upon the blackboard of our hearts the eternal lessons of sacrifice, service, surrender, duty, love and devotion. But like all students, those who serve within the sacred circle of the sanctuary can miss the lesson, can fail to understand the point of the teacher. If they are to be taught by their act of service, formed by its gift, then they must prepare themselves prayerfully for such formation and spiritual transformation. And before they depart from their work, they will spend time in thanksgiving for the refinement of the heart that has taken place in their service and for the resulting gift of closer union with God. These periods of personal preparation and gratitude will be times alone with the Lord who has called each to his or her special vocation of servanthood. Furthermore, the sacredness of our service can easily be forgotten while we are busy with the material concerns, the details of worship or service. Yet our actions, whether they are directly related to the altar or flow from it in service, are all times of prayer. As such, these times of service in themselves are intended to shape our hearts after the model of the heart of our Lord.

Within the mysterious plan of God, it is the spiritual transformation of every servant of God that is primarily intended, and only of secondary value is the liturgical or charitable service that is performed. God does not need our sacrifices, nor does the Divine Mystery find pleasure in ritual. Only in hearts and lives that increasingly are dedicated with devotion and love is the Divine Being delighted.

NOTE ON THE FOLLOWING PRAYERS

The prayers in this book (with the exception of those found on pages 94 and 103) are addressed to the First Person of the Trinity. The title *Lord* is used as it was by the ancient writer of the Psalms and as it has been cherished through the ages in the richness of our Judeo-Christian tradition.

PRAYER RITUALS
FOR A GATHERING
OF SERVANTS
BEFORE AND AFTER
THE SACRED LITURGY
OF THE EUCHARIST

COMMON PRAYER RITUAL
OF PREPARATION (1)

CELEBRANT:
Friends and fellow servants of God
    we are about to begin this Sacred Liturgy.
Let us each be mindful of the dignity that is ours
    and of the responsibility for making
    what we are about to do
    truly prayerful, sincere and beautiful.

Let us in the silence of our hearts
    ask the help of our Lord
    that we may each prayerfully carry out
    our personal responsibilities in this Sacred Liturgy:

individual prayers of preparation (pp. 24-44)

Lord, you have heard our personal prayers
    for each of the duties for which we are responsible.
May Your Holy Spirit rest upon us
    and guide us in all that we shall do.
May this Sacred Celebration
    give You glory, honor and praise.

Come, friends and fellow servants of God;
    let us begin in the name of the Father,
    and of the Son, and of the Holy Spirit.

Amen +

COMMON PRAYER RITUAL
OF THANKSGIVING (1)

*CELEBRANT: (Deacon or Lay Minister
if celebrant is greeting people)*

Lord, the Mass is ended,
    and before we remove our vestments,
    we pause to thank You
    for the honor of serving You
    and our brothers and sisters in the parish.

We are mindful, Gracious Lord,
    that our service does not stop
    when we leave this church,
    so we each pray a silent prayer to You:

individual prayers of thanksgiving (pp. 25-45)

addressing fellow servants:

In the name of the parish-community,
    I thank each of you for your generous service.
May God in the fullness of the Divine Heart,
    bless, reward and be ever present to each of you.
In the name of the Father,
    and of the Son, and of the Holy Spirit.

Amen +

COMMON PRAYER OF PREPARATION (2)

CELEBRANT: My friends,
all is now ready for the celebration.
The candles have been lighted, the music is prepared,
the Altar is in readiness.
May we now pause and, in silence, ask for Divine Aid
so that the action we are about to perform
will truly be honest and holy.
Let each pray his or her own prayer of preparation:

individual prayers of preparation (pp. 24-44)

Mindful of our human weakness, we join in common prayer:
*(To each intention, other servants may respond: LORD,
HEAR OUR PRAYER.)*

That our worship will flow from our hearts,
we pray to the Lord.

That our ministry at God's Altar be free of vanity,
we pray to the Lord.

That we become, even in our mistakes,
true instruments of the Grace of God,
we pray to the Lord.

Supported by prayer, inspired by the Holy Spirit,
let us proceed in peace
and in the name of our Lord, Jesus Christ.

Amen +

COMMON PRAYER OF THANKSGIVING (2)

CELEBRANT (or other):
Friends and fellow servants of God,
   in the Divine Wisdom, we have each been chosen
   by God and by this parish-community
   to serve at the Sacred Altar.
Let us not treat such an honor lightly
   but rather with a sincere expression of thanksgiving.
Let us each silently pray a prayer of gratitude:

individual prayers of thanksgiving (pp. 25-45)

Lord, we are eager to be on our way.
Have patience and help us take the proper time
   to thank You, our God and Source of our Life.
As we have served You here in the midst
   of the beauty and splendor of this Sacred Ceremony,
   may we serve You in that same spirit
   in each of the tasks of our lives.
May those lives proclaim to all—that we are
   servants of the sanctuary, servants of holiness,
   indeed, servants of God.

addressing fellow servants:

In the name of the parish and of the global Church
   whose worship we have helped celebrate, I thank you
   and ask that God will bless your comings and goings,
   your work, your home and your families,
   in the name of the Father, Son, and Holy Spirit.

Amen +

INDIVIDUAL PRAYERS
FOR SERVANTS
BEFORE AND AFTER
THE SACRED LITURGY
OF THE EUCHARIST

PRAYER OF PREPARATION
FOR A CELEBRANT

Lord of Hosts, the Power of Your Spirit is upon me
    and I am humbled by Your choice of me
    to be Your servant and friend.
As I now prepare to stand at Your Altar-Table,
    to be the celebrant of this Sacrifice,
    I am aware of the needs of my heart.
Gift me, I pray,
    with the fullness of the Divine Heart
    that I may truly be a minister of Truth.
Flow through me, I pray,
    with the vitality of endless ages,
    with the flaming fire of Pentecost
    and with the gentle strength of Your Son, Jesus.

Those who have come to this Celebration
    are hungry for Your Word,
    thirsty for Your Love
    and eager for the touch of Your Power.
May I empty myself of my self
    so that Your Word, Your Love, Your Touch,
    may stream through me.
May my attitude and my expression of reverence,
    reveal to those who are to serve with me,
    and to those who will worship with us,
    that You, our Lord and God, are among us.

Come Lord,
    help Your servant to truly be
    Your Servant.

Amen +

PRAYER OF THANKSGIVING
FOR A CELEBRANT

Lord God, I am tired—the demands have been many,
  and much of my energy is now drained.
Yet I am grateful for Your Presence
  in the midst of this Sacred Action
  and for the opportunity to serve that has been mine.

At the same time I am fearful
  that I will not be able to live out in my own life
  the words of the ritual that I have voiced.
Help me to truly give of myself, body and blood,
  as Your Son, Jesus, gave Himself to all.
May my life, even in its most remote corners,
  become what I have just celebrated.
Stretch me out, O Lord,
  to the limits of my gifts,
  to the outermost reaches
  of my powers to love and serve,
  so that the next time I approach Your Altar,
  I will be more worthy than I have been today.

With gratitude and devotion,
  I thank You for gifting me with Your Priesthood.

Amen +

PRAYER OF PREPARATION FOR A DEACON
OR A LAY MINISTER OF THE EUCHARIST

Lord, as the apostle John stood next to Your Son's Cross,
   so I am privileged to stand
   next to Your Altar-Table
   and serve in the Holy Sacrifice of the Mass.
In a long tradition of priestly people,
   I am grateful for the honor that is mine.

May my behavior and the attitude of my heart
   reflect that holy honor
   as I strive to serve in a sacred way.
With awe and wonder, I will hold in my hands
   the Body of Christ and His Sacred Blood,
   so that my sisters and brothers
   may be fed with the Food of Life.
Make my heart and hands clean.
Free me from anything of vanity and pride
   that might divorce me and the service that is mine
   from the heart of the Divine Mystery
   residing in this Holy Meal.

May I, with Your Constant Assistance,
   truly wait upon You and Your people
   in this Holy Liturgy of Praise and Adoration.

Amen +

PRAYER OF THANKSGIVING FOR A DEACON OR A LAY MINISTER OF THE EUCHARIST

Most High Lord, I have cared (am about to care)
    for the sacred vessels of Your Altar.
    and have seen (will see) that all is in order.
But this Liturgy is not ended,
    for its echo is in my heart,
    its fingerprints upon my hands,
    so that my whole life must reflect
    the dignity that has been mine
    through participating in this Holy Meal.

May those who see me at work or at play
    find nothing in my behavior that would detract
    from the sacred service I have just performed.
May my ministry of service continue,
    at home, at work
    and at the numerous crossroads of my life.
May I seek by personal prayer and acts of sacrifice
    to become the Living Body of Christ.

Thank You, my Lord,
    for the honor and responsibility of this sacred duty.

Amen +

PRAYER OF PREPARATION
FOR A LECTOR OR READER OF THE WORD

Lord, invest me with Your Power
   as I prepare to proclaim
   the Marvel of Your Message.
I have prepared my readings,
   I have tried to take within me
   the meaning of what I am about to read;
   help me, I ask, to read not just with my lips
   but with my whole heart and soul.

Lord, make me a hollow reed
   so that Your Voice will be heard
   by all who will hear me.
Free me of excessive concern over my performance,
   over the impression I create in this Sacred Action.
Convert my feelings of nervousness,
   turn all my apprehensions into an energy
   for proclaiming Your Word with power and authority.

May Your Spirit fill me
   as it fills the holy words
   that I am about to proclaim.

Amen +

PRAYER OF THANKSGIVING
FOR A LECTOR OR READER OF THE WORD

My Lord and Source of Divine Wisdom,
   Womb of the Word
   which I have been gifted to read
   to my brothers and sisters,
   help me as I now return to my daily duties,
   to live out in the fullest
   what I have proclaimed as Truth,
   what I have heralded as the Way and the Life.

I ask that my life may be an open gospel
   to all who observe my actions.
May my speech echo the Love of God,
   speak of the Lord's Generosity and Patience.
Lord, what I ask is that I might become Your Word
   to my family and to all whom I encounter.

May this request be granted
   in Your Divine and Compassionate Mercy,
   through Jesus Christ, my Brother and Lord.

Amen✝

PRAYER OF PREPARATION
FOR AN ACOLYTE

Lord, I ask that You would spark my memory
    to recall how Your Son, Jesus, at the first Mass
    did serve those who were at table with Him
    in the act of washing their feet.
May my service at this Mass be in that same style;
    may I with a humble yet proud heart
    serve the needs of the Table of the Lord.

Be with me as I stand at Your Table,
    so that my very attitude and behavior
    may be filled with diligence and dignity.
May nothing I do, by action or attitude,
    take away from the beauty and blessedness
    of this Sacred Action.

With humble gratitude for the privilege
    of serving at the Altar-Table,
    I prepare my heart to worship You
    as we are now about to begin this Holy Eucharist.

Amen +

PRAYER OF THANKSGIVING
FOR AN ACOLYTE

My Everlasting Lord,
   as I extinguish the candles at Your Table,
   may their flames burn brightly in my heart.
May the words, deeds and actions of my daily life
   make clear to others that I know
   that I have been privileged to serve You, my God,
   and my brothers and sisters
   in the Community of Christ.
May I be eager to serve Christ and others
   whenever I find them in need—
   in my home and family, in my daily activities—
   in every corner of life.

I make this request
   in the name of my Savior and Lord, Jesus Christ,
   who lives with You and the Spirit, forever and ever.

Amen +

PRAYER OF PREPARATION
FOR A MUSICIAN

Lord, the time is at hand;
  I am about to become Your sacred instrument.
Through me and the talents You have given me,
  I am about to become a channel
  of Your Mysterious Grace.
May the melody and song of this Celebration
  give honor to You, my God and Lord.
Free of excessive nervousness and fear,
  forgetful of myself,
  may I become a perfectly tuned instrument
  through which You mysteriously will touch
  each person who will hear the music
  that has been prepared.

Free my heart of pride
  and of any desire for attention
  so that the Divine Melody
  may be heard beneath each song,
  beneath every expression of my talent.
May this sacred worship be not a performance
  but my prayer to You,
  my service to the community
  and my gratitude for the gifts and talents
  that You have bestowed on me.

I am Yours, play upon me.

Amen ✛

PRAYER OF THANKSGIVING
FOR A MUSICIAN

Lord and God, the Liturgy is ended but the song goes on.
I thank You for the Grace of Your Presence
 and for Your direction of the music
 of this Celebration.

The applause for my music is heard only in heaven.
I am grateful that in some small way
 the hearts of those who came to worship
 were lifted to prayer by the expression of my gifts.

May my whole life be a harmonious song
 of gratitude for all that has been given me.
May my service, both to friends and family,
 contain the Melody of Your Divine Heart.
I thank You for the honor of serving others
 by being Your instrument of beauty and harmony.

I make this prayer through our Lord, Jesus Christ,
 who lives with You and the Holy Spirit forever.

Amen✝

PRAYER OF PREPARATION FOR AN ORGANIST

My Lord,
    soon my fingers will touch the organ keys,
    and music will begin to flow out in service
    to those who come to pray and to worship.
I have prepared and practiced this music,
    but the melody that touches the spirit
    must pour out from my heart
    and not merely from my hands and feet.

As this organ is but an instrument in my hands,
    may I become an instrument in Your Divine Hands,
    so that the music of this celebration
    may be harmonious with the Grace of Your Presence.

I am indeed grateful
    for the privilege and honor
    of serving my community and You, my Lord,
    with the ministry of making music.
Help me to be truly an instrument of Your Harmony.

Amen +

PRAYER OF THANKSGIVING FOR AN ORGANIST

Lord, the organ is now silent
    but my heart resonates with the song of service
    and the melody of gratitude.

I thank You for the gifts and talents
    with which You have blessed me.
I thank You for the great opportunity
    to use those talents for the glory of the Kingdom
    in the splendor of this Celebration now ended.
May my personal life reflect this gratitude,
    and may the haunting melody of Your Love
    ever resound in the depths of my heart
    and in all the work of my hands.

Amen +

PRAYER OF PREPARATION
FOR A CANTOR OR CHOIR MEMBER

Lord of Life, I pause in prayer
   before the beginning of this service.
Fill my voice with love for You.
May the notes that will sound
   find their harmony as they pass through my heart.
May the song of my mouth
   be a hymn of praise to You.

May I seek by my voice
   to give glory to You
   rather than to bring attention to myself.
May I seek humble service to the parish-community
   by the sharing of this gift
   with which You, my Lord, have blessed me.
Use me, Lord of Rhythm and Harmony,
   as You would play upon a hollow reed
   so that those whom I am called to serve
   may be attuned to Your Spirit and moved to prayer.

May my gift of service
   truly be my prayer to You this day.

Amen✝

PRAYER OF THANKSGIVING
FOR A CANTOR OR CHOIR MEMBER

Lord, I thank You for the privilege of serving others
   through Your great gift of song.
Yet I am aware that You can touch hearts
   with a baby's cry or the song of a bird.
So keep me humble in my service;
   keep me grateful in the use of my gifts;
   may the melody of Your Love linger long in my heart,
   and always resound in giving glory to You.

May the song of Your Son, Jesus,
   ring out not only from my lips
   but in everything I do.

May my whole life be a hymn of praise to You.

Amen ✝

PRAYER OF PREPARATION
FOR A SERVANT INVOLVED IN SACRED DANCE

Lord God,
　　You who are called Lord of the Dance,
　　animate my body, indeed my whole being,
　　with Your Living Spirit
　　so that I may express through my dance-worship
　　the balance and harmony of Your Creation.

As David danced before the Ark
　　in a gesture that was pleasing to You,
　　may my sacred movements also give glory to You.
May the prayer of dance that I perform
　　be a source of inspiration and devotion
　　for all who share in it.

May there be nothing in my attitude or behavior
　　to offend or divide those who have come here
　　to be united in a communion that is holy.
Release my body from the grip of tensions,
　　free my mind of nervousness and inhibition,
　　and empty my heart of self concern,
　　so that I may truly move
　　in Your Sacred Rhythm,
　　with the spontaneity of a young child
　　and the naturalness of a dancing leaf.

May this prayer come to You
　　through the merit of our Lord, Jesus Christ.

Amen +

PRAYER OF THANKSGIVING
FOR A SERVANT INVOLVED IN SACRED DANCE

I thank You, Boundless Lord,
    for the gifts with which You have graced me—
    I accept them in humility,
    mindful of my responsibility to use them always
    in the name of gracefulness, harmony and service.

May the dance of my daily life
    clearly point to Your Life-Giving Presence
    in all things and in every situation,
    just as my part
    in the sacred movement of this Celebration,
    has proclaimed the dance of all creation,
    of all the cosmos.
May I ever move in the harmony
    of stars and planets, earth and seas,
    as I strive to serve You in all I meet.

I ask this in the name of our Lord, Jesus Christ,
    who lives and moves with You
    in the unity of the Holy Spirit,
    now and forever.

Amen +

PRAYER OF PREPARATION FOR AN USHER

Lord of the Eternal Feast,
　　it is about time for me to begin my holy duty
　　as an usher at this Celebration.
Help me to perform this duty with dignity
　　for I represent not only this parish-community
　　but Your Kingdom and Your very Person.

Remind me of how our Lord Jesus
　　was offended by a lack of proper courtesy
　　when He came to the house of the pharisee.
May no one,
　　stranger or friend, fellow parishioner or guest,
　　have any reason to be offended
　　by a lack of kindness or courtesy on my part.

May I, with reverence and friendliness, welcome all.
May I, with attention and diligence,
　　care for the needs of the community as it worships.
May my prayer during this Sacred Action
　　be that of watchfulness
　　and the desire to serve others.

I ask, Lord, that You smile through me,
　　that You greet through my hospitality
　　and that You may be made visible to me
　　in all to whom I serve.

Amen✝

PRAYER OF THANKSGIVING FOR AN USHER

Lord, my God,
    the Celebration is finished and the pews are empty.
As I prepare to return to my home and family,
    may I, by Your Grace,
    usher-in the Kingdom
    by my life and my work.
Help me to be a holy person;
    help me to see You
    in each person I shall meet,
    in family and friend and the stranger as well.

As I seek to serve you with honor and holiness,
    grant me and those whom I love,
    a seat at Your Heavenly Banquet...
    where all who struggle to serve You,
    without regard to status or position,
    shall be ushered to You by Your Son and His Mother.

I ask this through our Lord, Jesus Christ,
    who lives with You and the Spirit, forever and ever.

Amen ✝

PRAYER OF PREPARATION
FOR A SERVANT COUNTING MONEY

Lord, before I take an account of the gifts
    that Your people have offered
    to You and to our community,
    I pause to be in communion with You
    so that I may see in this task that is necessary
    one that is holy as well.
I ask that Matthew, gospel writer and money counter,
    show to me that all is holy in Your Kingdom
    and that each task surrounding the Liturgy is sacred.

I have been entrusted by my brothers and sisters
    with this my service-duty.
May it truly be my prayer to You, O Lord.
Make me mindful in this accounting of gifts,
    of the way in which I am of service
    to the parish-community and to all
    who will benefit from these gifts of charity.

Matthew,
    saint of money counters and followers of Christ,
    be with me as I begin,
    in the name of the Father, Son, and Holy Spirit.

Amen +

PRAYER OF THANKSGIVING
FOR A SERVANT COUNTING MONEY

Bountiful Lord, my work is finished,
   and the gifts of Your people
   are now counted and recorded.

I am grateful to have been chosen for this service.
May this work be my gift-offering to You.

As the generosity of others has passed through my hands,
   may the touch of that generosity
   find expression in my daily life,
   with my family and friends
   and with the stranger as well.

Bless me and the work of my hands,
   in Your Holy Name:
   Father, Son, and Holy Spirit.

Amen +

PREPARATION PRAYER FOR A SERVANT WHO PREPARES THE SANCTUARY

Lord, God of Hosts,
    Your Son, Jesus, sent His disciples ahead of Him
    to prepare all things for the Passover Meal,
    for the event of His Last Supper.
Like them I have been given the honor
    of preparing the special place
    where the memory of that Sacred Meal will be relived.

May my concern
    for the prayerfulness of these surroundings,
    for the order and neatness of this sacred space,
    for the holy vessels and all that is needed,
    be my prayerful preparation for this time of worship.
May I not approach this holy service as a mere task
    but see in it the opportunity to serve You, Lord,
    as well as the community of worshipers
    and the other ministers of the Altar.

May the work that I am about to perform,
    while unseen by many,
    be a source of visible glory and honor to You.

I ask this through our Lord Jesus Christ,
    who lives with You and the Spirit, forever and ever.

Amen ✝

THANKSGIVING PRAYER FOR A SERVANT WHO PREPARES THE SANCTUARY

Beloved Lord,
    I have carefully returned each thing
    to its proper place.
Once again all is quiet.
I treasure these opportunities of serving others
    in my necessary but unseen work.
You are a God who sees what is done in private;
    reward me only with a longing to love You more.

May the holy things that I have touched
    leave a living imprint on me
    so that I may seek holiness
    in every corner of my life.
Call forth from within me
    a desire to serve You always in hidden but holy ways.

May this task that I have just finished
    advance Your Kingdom
    and add to the growth of my holiness.

I ask this through our Lord, Jesus Christ,
    who lives and reigns with You
    in the unity of the Holy Spirit,
    forever and ever.

Amen ✝

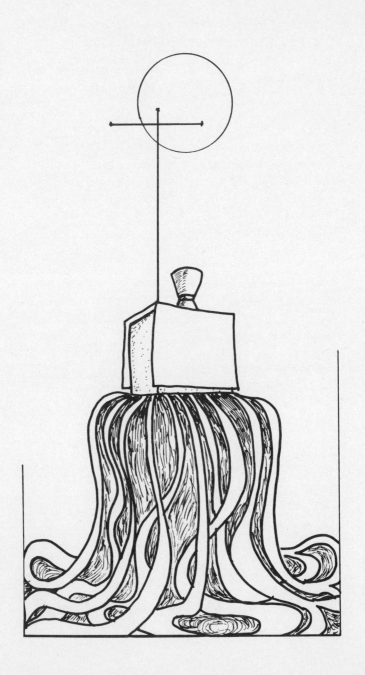

PRAYERS FOR SERVANTS
WHOSE MINISTRY
FLOWS FROM THE ALTAR

PREPARATION PRAYER
FOR A MINISTER OF A COMMUNION SERVICE
OUTSIDE OF THE HOLY EUCHARIST

Lord, my God,
    in the absence of our pastor and spiritual leader,
    I am to preside over this time
    of prayer and communion with You.
Help me to lead this service
    not only by my presence
    but by the holiness of my life.

Remove from me any barriers to Your Grace
    so that, through me, others may be nourished.
May my attention to the ritual of this sacred time,
    especially in my reverence and devotion,
    be what You desire from those
    who are called to serve at Your Altar-Table.

Nourish me, Lord, with Your Blessing,
    as I now begin this worship service
    in the name of the Father, Son, and Holy Spirit.

Amen +

THANKSGIVING PRAYER
FOR A MINISTER OF A COMMUNION SERVICE
OUTSIDE OF THE HOLY EUCHARIST

I thank You, Gracious God,
   that through my hands
   You have entered the lives of Your people,
   nourished their dreams of holiness
   and have been for them, the Food of Life.

Touch me with that same strength
   and aid me as I strive to find holiness
   according to my lifework
   and in my devotion to You.
May I be both gospel and holy food
   for all whom I meet.

I ask this in the name of Your Son, Jesus Christ,
   who lives and reigns with You
   in the unity of the Holy Spirit,
   now and forever.

Amen +

PREPARATION PRAYER
FOR A SERVANT WHO TAKES COMMUNION
TO THE SICK OR ELDERLY

My Lord and Sustainer of All Beings,
 I kneel here before the Sacred Presence
 about to take the Bread of Life
 to those who are unable to attend
 the communal Celebration of the Eucharist.
It will be my honor to carry Christ to them.

Bless my hands that they may be
 fitting instruments of this Holy Visitation.
Bless my heart, that I may truly carry Your Spirit
 in carrying the Bread of Life to those
 whose spirits are in need.

Make me aware
 that all I shall encounter on my sacred journey
 will be blessed by the Divine Presence.
May my attitude, my reverence and my concern
 for both the spiritual and material needs
 of those whom I shall visit
 be that of Your Divine Heart.

I ask this in the name of our Lord, Jesus Christ,
 whose Body and Blood I shall carry;
 He who lives with You and the Holy Spirit
 forever and ever.

Amen +

THANKSGIVING PRAYER
FOR A SERVANT WHO TAKES COMMUNION
TO THE SICK OR ELDERLY

Divine Source of Life and Health,
    I thank You for the honor and privilege
    of being a Christ-bearer.
As I have carried the Sacred Presence
    to those who have received Holy Communion,
    may I carry within my own person
    that same Presence to all I meet,
    to family and friends, to the stranger and to the world.
May my whole life proclaim
    that I carry my Lord day and night
    within the vessel of my heart.

I lift up into Your Divine Heart
    the needs of those whom I have visited;
    be with each of them and especially with _____,
    who is in need of Your Continuous Presence.

I bow before You, my Lord and God,
    grateful that You have chosen me to serve You
    and my brothers and sisters.

Amen +

PREPARATION PRAYER FOR A SERVANT WHO ACTS AS A LEADER OF PRAYER

Divine Creator and Bountiful Lord,
    all Your creation rings out Your praise.
From the beginning,
    a continuous canticle of prayer
    has risen to You from all the earth,
    from all the universe.

I have been asked to set in motion that flow of prayer
    here in this place and this time.
I have been invited to serve You and others
    as a leader of prayer.
Come then, Lord,
    and make my heart a shrine of prayer.
Bring me to that place of awe within
    where I can be a living prayer.

May I take confidence in the truth
    that in choosing Your servants You cherish them,
    and You gift them with Your Divine Spirit.
Surrounded and inspired by that Spirit,
    I will give You honor in my service of leadership.

May the prayer that I lead
    be in perfect harmony with the prayers
    that rise from all peoples on this earth
    and with the ancient prayers of all creation.
With trust and devotion,
    I place myself into Your Loving Hands.

Amen +

THANKSGIVING PRAYER FOR A SERVANT
WHO ACTS AS A LEADER OF PRAYER

Thank You, Holy Lord,
    for the gifts of prayer that have been ours
    during this time of worship.
Thank You, God of Jacob,
    for the gift of servanthood that has been mine,
    for the beautifully humbling experience
    of having been a channel for Your Holy Presence.

May I, by my life, pray always
    by working, living and loving in that Presence.
    The cosmos is Your Temple;
    may I lead prayer within that larger Temple
    by all that I do.

I make this prayer
    in the name of Your Son, our Lord, Jesus Christ.

Amen✛

PREPARATION PRAYER FOR A SERVANT VISITING THE SICK OR ELDERLY

Compassionate Lord,
    I am about to begin my work of service
    to You and to the parish-community
    and to be its representative in Your Name
    as I go forth to visit.
Mindful of the journey of the Virgin Mary
    to call upon her cousin Elizabeth,
    I ask that this work of mine
    be truly a Visitation.
May You, my Lord and God,
    visit those I will see,
    using me as Your vessel of visitation.

Empty my heart
    so that it will be filled with You.
Humble me
    and remove all that may prevent You, my Lord,
    from being the Gift that I will bring to them.
May my words be honest and real
    so that they may be channels for Your Grace.
Through Your Continuous Assistance,
    I will strive to give myself in service
    but never impose myself upon those I visit.

Finally, Lord, make me conscious
    of how it is I
    who will be visited by You
    as I enter into the sacred circles
    of sickness, loneliness and old age.

Amen ✝

THANKSGIVING PRAYER FOR A SERVANT VISITING THE SICK OR ELDERLY

Gentle and Consoling Lord,
  I thank You for the honor of serving You
  through this my work of visitation.
I am thankful for the health of body and spirit,
  for the freedom of movement,
  with which You have blessed me.

I am thankful for the many ways I have been touched
  by the lives of those whom I have visited.
I pray now for each of them and their needs.
I especially lift up into Your Divine Heart
  the needs of _____.

May I carry this spirit of prayer and service
  into every corner of my day-to-day life.
Lord, visit me daily with Your Peace,
  now and at the hour of my death.

Amen +

PREPARATION PRAYER
FOR A SERVANT VISITING THE SICK

Lord, Divine Healer,
   fill my heart with Your Compassion
   as I begin the prayerful work of visiting
   those whom You have visited with sickness.

May my presence be a healing.
May my presence be a sign
   of the parish-community of which they are a part
   and of the global Church to which they belong.
Even, Lord, to those who are not of my community,
   may my being among them,
   in my respect and reverence for their sickness,
   be a blessing and a Divine Visitation.
Guide me, I ask,
   so that all I do and say may be honest and holy.

I ask this through the Redeeming Grace
   of Your Son, our Lord, Jesus Christ.

Amen+

THANKSGIVING PRAYER
FOR A SERVANT VISITING THE SICK

Merciful Lord,
  my ministry of visitation is now ended,
  but my ministry of prayer only begins.
As I was present to those I visited
  in humility and respect for their illness,
  may I now be present with them
  before You in prayer.
I place before You the needs of each person: _____.

They have placed their trust in You, O Lord;
  look with kindness upon their faith
  and grant them health, holiness
  and the gift of Your Abiding Presence.

I ask this with confidence
  in the name of Your Son, Jesus Christ,
  who lives with You and the Holy Spirit,
  now and forever.

Amen +

PREPARATION PRAYER
FOR A DIRECTOR OF RELIGIOUS EDUCATION

Lord, Divine Source of All Truth,
   I have been called by You
   into the ministry of love.
We can not love what we do not know;
   by my service to the parish and to all the world,
   may others come to love You with greater devotion
   because they have come to know You more.

As You, my God, have made Yourself known
   through the service of prophets and holy people,
   and through the ministry of Your Son, Jesus,
   may I too be a living sign of Your Love,
   a window to the wonder of Your Presence.

Come and be with me in the midst of daily duties
   that often seem so routine or difficult.
Teach me, Lord, that You reveal Yourself
   in what seems to be failure as well as in success
   so that I may, with confidence,
   do all things out of love for You.
With such an awareness,
   my joy will come in service rather than in success.

I ask this of You in the name of Your Son, Jesus Christ,
   who lives with You and the Holy Spirit,
   forever and ever.

Amen ✝

THANKSGIVING PRAYER
FOR A DIRECTOR OF RELIGIOUS EDUCATION

Lord, my God,
   the work of this day is done,
   and I thank You for all the gifts that it has held.
At the same time, I know that much remains to be done
   if those who need to know of You
   are to be nourished by instruction in Your Way
   and endowed with the gift of Your Divine Wisdom.
Invest me with Your Great Gift of Patience
   so that I may await without anxiety
   all that remains to be completed.
And although at times the work of my ministry
   may leave me physically and mentally drained,
   refresh me with the awareness
   that my small efforts of this day
   have caused the Kingdom to come that much sooner.

Endless Source of True Wisdom,
   remind me of the words of Your Son, Jesus,
   that whoever fulfills and teaches Your Commands
   shall be great in the Kingdom of God.
May the greatness I seek be measured by my service,
   and may my service in the ministry of holy learning
   not be measured merely by the clock.

Help me, Your servant,
   to live out all that I have tried to set in motion,
   and renew me in my dedication with Your Great Love
   for all the tomorrows of my ministry.

Amen✝

PREPARATION PRAYER
FOR A TEACHER OF RELIGION

Divine Source of All Wisdom and Truth,
  I come before You asking Your Blessed Aid
  as I prepare to teach in Your Name.
I am aware that I have been called and selected
  by You and Your Church
  and that with that calling
  comes the necessary courage and grace,
  but I ask Your Special Help
  so that I may open myself
  to each situation in this class
  in such a way that I may truly be
  a teacher in the pattern of Jesus.
Help me to reverence those I teach, as He did—
Help me to love those whom I instruct,
  as He loved His disciples—
Help me to speak to their hearts
  as well as to their heads
  and to touch them with the devotion and dedication
  of my own life lived in You.

I am humbled, my Lord,
  when I realize that I am the textbook
  from which they will learn the most.
Help me, Lord, to be gentle yet firm,
  loving yet strong,
  patient yet challenging.
Come Lord and accompany me as I begin to teach
  in the name of the Father, Son, and Holy Spirit.

Amen +

THANKSGIVING PRAYER
FOR A TEACHER OF RELIGION

The students, Lord, have left,
    and I thank You for Your Continuous Presence
    in my class.
That Presence has been a constant reminder
    of the real purpose of my presence among them:
    to be a teacher of Truth.

The challenge of that calling reminds me
    that I must, by prayer and service,
    transform my life
    into a revelation of You, my Lord and God.
Being the gospel is far from easy,
    yet it is a challenge that I embrace
    since it is my privilege and grace
    to fulfill the admonition of Your Son, Jesus,
    to "teach all nations."

Nourish my lacking spirit,
    remove my doubts
    and help those students
    who are in need of Your Love,
    who search for Your Light and Your Strength.

Gracious God, be with them and with me.

Amen✝

PREPARATION PRAYER
FOR A YOUTH WORKER

My Lord and God,
    before I begin this _____ (activity),
    part of my ministry to the youth,
    I come to You seeking Your Blessing.
Help me to proclaim,
    not by words, but by the dedication of my heart,
    the realness of Your Kingdom.

As I concern myself
    with the practical necessities of this event,
    keep me attuned to the needs of those I serve.
Open my third eye
    so that I may see beyond the surface behavior
    of those who are crying out for help,
    and grant me a listening ear.

May I at all times proclaim
    the values and principles for which I stand.
May I never water down the high ideals of the Gospels
    just so that I myself may be accepted.
May I, with humility, deep love and humor
    strive to be Your servant
    and a servant of the community.

In peace and confidence,
    I begin in the name of the Father,
    and of the Son,
    and of the Holy Spirit.

Amen +

THANKSGIVING PRAYER
FOR A YOUTH WORKER

Remind me, Lord and Source of True Wisdom,
    that success must be seen through Your Divine Eyes
    and that You work in mysterious ways—
    in seeming successes
    and in apparent failures, as well.
You seek individual hearts and not crowds,
    and numbers have never been a scale
    for measuring Your Divine Presence.

I thank You for the opportunity that has been mine
    and ask that with Your Holy Help,
    I may allow my work and service
    to be a source of personal growth in holiness.
Lord, challenge me to greatness and to excellence
    in this service to Your youth.
And may I see that holy challenge
    in all of my day-to-day life.

I ask this through my Lord and Brother, Jesus Christ.

Amen ✝

PREPARATION PRAYER FOR A SERVANT BEARING GIFTS OF AID TO THOSE IN NEED

Bountiful Lord,
   I am to serve You and my brothers and sisters
   by being the messenger of Your Kindness.
Help me to bring this expression of concern
   to those who are in need—
   in the spirit of Your Son, Jesus Christ.

May there be nothing in my attitude or behavior
   to cause those who are to receive these gifts
   to be embarrassed or ashamed.
May I wrap these gifts
   in humility, respect and kindness
   as I prayerfully serve You, my God, through them.
Remove from me any attitude of superiority,
   since it is not the well-off helping those in need,
   but only Christ serving Christ.
In the unity of His Body we are all one,
   let my attitude reflect my belief
   in this profound truth.

Open my heart
   to accept any expressions of gratitude—
   as well as any lack of gratitude
   which is so often but a defense to hide shame.

Help me, Lord,
   as I begin this service of prayerful charity
   in the name of the Father, Son, and Holy Spirit.

Amen +

THANKSGIVING PRAYER FOR A SERVANT BEARING GIFTS OF AID TO THOSE IN NEED

Generous Lord, it is I who have been gifted
   by this opportunity to serve.
I am grateful that I have been allowed
   to represent the community,
   the larger Church and You
   in the work I have done.

Make me increasingly mindful of all who are in need.
May I seek to serve the poor
   and their needs of both body and spirit,
   with natural, humble and holy service.
Make me more and more mindful of my own poverty
   and my need of You.

May this work that I have just performed
   be a true prayer to You.
May my service ever give You glory and honor.

I ask this through Jesus Christ, our Lord and Healer.

Amen +

PREPARATION PRAYER FOR A SERVANT DEMONSTRATING FOR SOCIAL JUSTICE

Lord, send me the gift of Your Holy Spirit,
    so that I may perceive this issue
    in the full light of Your Divine Plan.
Humble me so that I do not become
    a victim of self-righteousness
    but rather act as an instrument of service
    to the Church and to my community.
Drain my heart of the will to misuse power
    while attempting to achieve desired results.
Mindful of how our Lord, Jesus Christ,
    blessed those who persecuted Him,
    may I show only compassion, kindness and gentleness
    to all whom I will encounter.
May my love for even those who oppose what I believe in,
    be the symbol that all shall see.

Let me see that You, my God, often choose failure
    as the most effective means of achieving Your Will.
Allow me to embrace failure, if that be necessary,
    with the same devotion and confidence
    with which Christ embraced
    the apparent failure of His Cross.
Finally, Lord, remind me frequently
    that it is the peacemakers who are Your Children.
May this work that I now begin in Your Holy Name,
    advance the good of the Kingdom
    and my own holiness as well.

Amen +

THANKSGIVING PRAYER FOR A SERVANT DEMONSTRATING FOR SOCIAL JUSTICE

Lord and God,
    Your Son, Jesus, not only with words
    but with compassionate deeds
    that flowed from His communion with You,
    was a model for the social action
    in which I have just taken part.
May the resolution of that action
    help to call forth Your Peaceable Kingdom.

I place into Your Hands
    the success or failure of my service.
As a servant of the Kingdom of Justice and Peace,
    may I find my reward
    only in actions of true service.

I lift up into Your Heart
    the present situation that has made
    this social demonstration a necessity.

silent prayer

Lord, may my life be always
    a living sign of Your Compassionate Justice.
I ask this with confidence,
    through Jesus Christ, our Lord,
    who lives with You and the Holy Spirit,
    now and forever.

Amen ✝

PREPARATION PRAYER FOR A SERVANT WHO WORKS AT A SOCIAL EVENT

Gracious God,
   Your Son, Jesus, delighted in wedding feasts
   and in being invited to banquets.
May He, our Lord and Savior, be present to me
   as I serve our parish in preparation for _____.

On the surface, this work seems so ordinary,
   this event like so many mundane ones,
   that I can easily forget
   that it is prayerful service
   to all the community and so, also, to You.
May the many concerns
   about the practical aspects and needs of this gathering
   not hide the fact that it is meant to be prayer.

May we show respect to one another
   and bring glory to You,
   as we strive to work in harmony with each other.
May I find pleasure in this preparation,
   and salvation in my service to the Church.

I begin this work of service,
   in the name of the Father, and of the Son,
   and of the Holy Spirit.

Amen +

THANKSGIVING PRAYER FOR A SERVANT
WHO WORKS AT A SOCIAL EVENT

Lord, hear me;
  I am tired but do not want to leave
  until I have expressed my gratitude
  for the success of this event.

I thank You for the privilege
  of assisting others by my simple tasks.
This time of service has been my prayer to You.
May that spirit of service
  spread throughout my daily life.

All is finished,
  and as we prepare to depart, each to our homes,
  I ask Your Blessing
  upon our families, our parish, and upon each of us
  in the name of the Father,
  of the Son, and of the Holy Spirit.

Amen +

PRAYER FOR A SERVANT OF GOD (any ministry)

My Lord, God of Mystery and Awe,
  Your choice of servants amazes me.
You could have chosen
  from among those much more wise and talented,
  yet You have called upon me.

I am honored by this opportunity to be Your servant
  by being of service to my brothers and sisters.
In Your invitation to serve,
  I realize that I am drawn
  into a special relationship with You,
  my Lord and my God.
May this act of ministry of _____
  be for me a means of grace
  and of building up the Body of Christ.

May I serve with humility and honor
  seeking not my own advancement or self-acclaim
  but rather to give glory to You
  and to work for the coming of the Kingdom.
Help me, I pray, to do well—
  to do Your Will—
  in this ministry with which You have gifted me.

Amen ✝

PRAYER OF THANKSGIVING
AFTER A TIME OF SERVICE

Lord and Divine Friend,
 my task is completed,
 and I treasure this opportunity
 of having been invited into Your Service.

Grant that I may be open
 to the 10,000 daily invitations to be of service:
 to my family, my friends,
 to the stranger and the guest,
 and so to truly live up to the privilege
 of being called a servant of God.

I ask this of You, through Your Son, Jesus Christ,
 who lives with You and the Holy Spirit,
 forever and ever.

Amen+

PRAYER FOR
AN OFFICER ON A PARISH COUNCIL

My Lord and Source of All Strength,
   I ask Your Holy Help
   so that I might fittingly serve my community
   as an officer on the parish council.
May I, with faith and devotion,
   seek to serve my parish-community
   and the needs of the world that surrounds it.

Guide me, I pray, to truly represent
   not only those who chose me
   but above all, You and Your Kingdom.
May the truth of the Gospels
   be a light of insight for my decisions
   and a source of support in times of weakness.

And finally, with Your Divine Assistance,
   may I find in this role of servant
   a royal path to holiness,
   a true way to Your Heart,
   my Lord and my God.

Amen +

PRAYER FOR
A MEMBER OF A PARISH COUNCIL

My Lord and God,
    my ministry of service to my parish
    is also my service of You, my God.
May I find in this position of honor and trust,
    a renewal of my personal search for holiness.

Accept, as my prayer to You,
    the hours of service
    that I shall give.
Accept as my worship,
    the time, effort and work that is required
    of those who serve as I do.

Make of me
    an instrument of Your Will,
    as I attempt to meet the real needs
    of those who have chosen me as their representative.
Fill me with Your Holy Spirit
    so that, by my work and service,
    Your Kingdom will come,
    in fullness and in peace,
    to my parish-community.

Confident in Your Divine Help,
    supported by Your Son, Jesus,
    and enlightened by the Holy Spirit,
    may I serve You, my Lord,
    as I serve others.

Amen +

PRAYER FOR ANY ELECTED OFFICER

Lord,
    my time of service to others seems endless.
Help me to accept all that is involved
    in this ministry for which I have been chosen.
Continue to show to me
    how it is to be my prayer and devotion
    to You, my God.

Keep my heart open to the mystery
    of how You work within my life
    in the midst of such service
    as I now give to others.
Unlock to me, I pray,
    the secret of how in such a ministry
    honor, glory, and praise
    is indeed given to You.

As Your servant, I bow before You
    and the mystery of Your Holy Will.

Amen +

PRACTICE AND PREPARATION
AS PRAYER

The more practical the aspect of our lives, the less likely will it seem to lend itself to prayer. This is true even of the more practical aspects of the sacred liturgy. However, it is equally true that for a liturgy to be beautiful and harmonious, it is necessary to set aside time to work with the practical. Readers, musicians, those who serve about the altar—servants in each role—need to practice what they are to do for their actions to be graceful and natural. However necessary, we often fail to perceive that each time of preparation is an integral part of the sacred liturgy and therefore is deserving of a prayerful attitude.

Aware that our conception of time is much of the problem, we might find it helpful to consider all time as but a single moment where past, present and future are fused. Practice time is thus not separate from sacred time; rather, it is but the beginning of the action. Anticipation, celebration and thanksgiving form a trinity of prayer, and practice done with reverence and attention to detail and beauty cause the celebration of our service to flow naturally through each stage of our sacred action.

Proper preparation for any expresssion of the liturgy, for any service rendered to God and the Church, includes more than physical preparation. A thorough preparation will include the preparation of reshaping our hearts as well, and this preparation can begin at the practice time itself. The first step in this inner preparation can be the intention that nothing be done carelessly or cheaply. In this mindfulness, the rehearsal of movements, songs or readings can become the beginning of our holy work. But of primary importance in this work of reshaping the heart is a deeply abiding reverence for the place of our worship-practice and for the other persons involved in the preparation—all in the light of what we are doing and for whom we are doing it. If veneration for the altar, for the sacred space of the church, happens only when the community is gathered, then we can easily fall into duplicity, into the reverence of hypocrites. When humor is present, for example, let it be expressed in such a way that it heightens the experience of the Divine Presence and does not take away from that Presence. This is equally true in each way that we interact with our fellow servants in the course of the practice. The intention to heighten the experience of the Presence of God is, of course, the very goal of the sacred liturgy, and our desire to know His Presence—expressed in our attitude of reverence—will thus flow out into all our daily events. It is thus that the trinity of prayer is completed and that all the actions of sacred worship will touch the many corners of the universe and beyond.

May these prayers be an aid in our viewing even our preparation as a time of prayer and worship.

PRAYERS
FOR REHEARSAL
AND PREPARATION

PRAYER BEFORE A WEDDING REHEARSAL

Friends, before we begin our rehearsal, let us pray:

silent prayer

    _____(groom)_____ and _____(bride)_____ ,
family and friends of the bride and groom,
may we make this time of preparation
a part of the worship of the wedding.

May our practice be a pattern of prayer and devotion
that will shape the beauty and grace
of the ceremony of marriage between these two
who so love one another.
May the spirit of love which has united them
and brought them to this point in their lives
be the spirit that will surround
this entire time of preparation.

Let us begin our practice
in the name of our Lord, Jesus Christ,
who lives with You and the Holy Spirit,
forever and ever.

Amen +

PRAYER AFTER A WEDDING REHEARSAL

Before we depart from this church,
    let us again pause to pray:
Friends, we have been honored to share
    with   (groom)   and   (bride)   ,
    this most sacred moment of their marriage.
May this practice in which we have participated
    be part of that solemn dedication.
Let us pause now and ask that God will bless them
    with love and happiness all their lives:

silent prayer

Mindful, Lord,
    that our physical preparation of the ceremony
    is but a part of the solemn dedication,
    we ask that we be truly prepared in heart and spirit.
Remove from us all sin
    and all barriers to true worship of You, our God.
May nothing in our lives or in our hearts
    hinder the flow of Your Divine Grace.
Visit us, Lord of Compassion, with Your Mercy
    and unite all of us in love and peace.
We ask this through our Lord, Jesus Christ,
    who lives with You and the Holy Spirit,
    now and forever.

May we go in joy and in peace.

Amen ✛

PRAYER BEFORE A WEDDING REHEARSAL

Friends, as we begin this time of practice,
    let us pray:
Lord, You who created the mystery of human love
    and who takes great delight in marriage,
    be with us as we begin this time of rehearsal.
Our hearts are filled with joy
    at the happiness between
        _____(bride)_____   and   _____(groom)_____

    as they now practice the ceremony
    of their solemn and holy vows of marriage.

All of us are important to that sacred work.
Make us mindful that our preparation
    is part of the prayer of this marriage.
May we allow even our mistakes in this practice
    to be part of that prayer.
Keep all of us—
    family and friends,
    along with the members of the bridal party—
    ever mindful of that intention
    in the attitudes of our hearts.

May the reverence and respect,
    the devotion and prayerfulness of this practice,
    find its harvest fulfillment
    in the beauty and joy of the wedding celebration.

Let us begin this holy action in the name of the Father,
    and of the Son, and of the Holy Spirit.

Amen +

PRAYER AFTER A WEDDING REHEARSAL

Friends, we have with anticipation
   prepared for the Sacred Nuptials
   of ____(bride)____ and ____(groom)____ .
Keep us mindful, Lord,
   that external actions are not enough.
Let us also prepare our hearts
   so that together we may surround these two
   who so love one another
   with all the grace and love at hand.

Remove from us, Lord of Mercy,
   any thoughts, deeds or attitudes
   that might prevent us from entering fully
   into the joyful celebration of love and union.
We pause to search our hearts for sin or imperfections:

silent prayer

May the Mercy of our Compassionate God
   forgive us our failings and prepare our hearts.
Bless, O Lord, the joyfulness,
   the play and celebration of this time.

addressing people:

May God keep all of you safe
   and under the Divine Protection.

Go in peace, the rehearsal is over.

Amen +

PRAYER BEFORE A PRACTICE
FOR THE RECEPTION OF A SACRAMENT
(Holy Communion, Confirmation or other)

Let us pray:
May we be mindful as we practice for this Holy Sacrament
    that this time of rehearsal is, in itself, prayer.
May we pause now and be aware
    of the Divine Presence of our Lord and God:

silent prayer

Lord, be with us as we practice.
By this time of preparation we seek
    not only to learn correct movements and positions
    but to prepare our hearts
    for the Great Mystery that will soon be ours.

May we be attentive to the instructions that are given.
May we remember what is told to us
    so that all will be in harmony
    when we are to receive You.

Be with us, Lord,
    as we begin this practice in Your Sacred Sign:
    in the name of the Father,
    and of the Son, and of the Holy Spirit.

Amen +

PRAYER AFTER A PRACTICE
FOR THE RECEPTION OF A SACRAMENT
(Holy Communion, Confirmation or other)

Let us pray:
All is in readiness, Lord;
    we have practiced in preparation
    for Your Divine Visitation in the Sacrament of _____.
Now it is our task
    to properly prepare our hearts as well.
Let us remember all who will receive the Sacrament
    as we pause now in silence:

silent prayer

Let us also remember
    all who have prepared us for this sacred event: _____
    and all who support us with their affection and love: _____.

addressing candidates:

As you await the coming of God's Grace,
    may the Lord watch over you,
    may the Lord bless you,
    and fill your hearts with joy and happiness.

Let us depart now in the name of the Father,
    and of the Son, and of the Holy Spirit.

Amen +

PRAYER BEFORE A PRACTICE
FOR A LITURGICAL FUNCTION

CELEBRANT OR LEADER: Let us pause for prayer
before we begin this time of practice:

silent prayer

Lord, make us aware of Your Divine Presence
as we prepare for _____.
In order that this period of preparation
may be an integral part of the worship celebration,
let us surround it and ourselves
with a sense of reverence and deep respect.
May even our errors in this time of practice
give You glory and honor.

We ask that, by this prayerful preparation,
the ceremony itself will speak of Your Presence
to all who are a part of it.
By its beauty and correctness,
by the grace of its action,
may it be wordless worship of You, our Lord and God.

Amen +

PRAYER AFTER A PRACTICE
FOR A LITURGICAL FUNCTION

Lord, we have prepared the actions
   of the celebration that is to come:
   now let us prepare our hearts as well.

We thank You for the honor
   present in this practice
   of being able to serve You
   and the parish-community.
May our gratitude and appreciation
   form the heart of our prayer.

We ask this through our Lord, Jesus Christ,
   who lives with You, in the unity of the Holy Spirit,
   forever and ever.

Amen +

PRAYER BEFORE A PRACTICE
FOR A LITURGICAL FUNCTION

CELEBRANT or LEADER: Let us pray:
   Lord, before we begin this practice period,
   we ask that You keep us ever-mindful
   of the fact that we stand in Sacred Space.
May our behavior and our attitude
   reflect that we know where we are
   and whom we serve.
Be with us as we begin, in the name of the Father,
   and of the Son, and of the Holy Spirit.

Amen +

PRAYER AFTER A PRACTICE
FOR A LITURGICAL FUNCTION

Our Lord, we pray that our practice
   has truly been our prayer of preparation.
Remind us of all that this practice has shown us
   so that in all things
   we may give You honor and glory.
Let us pause now for silent prayer:

silent prayer

May we depart with the Blessing of God,
   in the name of the Father, Son, and Holy Spirit.

Amen +

PRAYER BEFORE A MUSIC PRACTICE

Help us, Lord,
    we who are Your ministers of music
    to be reverent and respectful
    in this time of practice.
May this prayer strike a note of consciousness
    of what we do and for whom we do it.
May all that we say and do,
    our laughter and our difficulties as well,
    form a hymn of honest praise
    that we offer to You.

May You, God of Harmony, be our director
    as we begin in the Sacred Name:
    Father, Son, and Holy Spirit.

Amen ✛

PRAYER AFTER A MUSIC PRACTICE

Lord, we may have praised You with some wrong notes
    but always with loving hearts.
We have given You glory by beautiful harmony
    as well as by the awareness
    of what we are preparing ourselves to perform.
Be with us now as we conclude
    in the name of the Father, Son, and Holy Spirit.

Amen ✛

PRAYER BEFORE A MUSIC PRACTICE

Let us pause to pray before we practice:

silent prayer

Help us, Lord, to be mindful
 that this preparation
 is part of the song of service—
 that even our practice is prayer.
And we ask that it may be done in that spirit.

May we be mindful of the responsibility that is ours
 to seek excellence by this rehearsal
 since it is You, our God, for whom we play.
May we seek to play with professional skill
 but even more with that perfection of heart
 by which all music reaches heaven.

In harmony with the purpose of our performance,
 let us practice prayerfully
 in the name of the Father, Son, and Holy Spirit.

Amen +

PRAYER AFTER A MUSIC PRACTICE

Lord,
   keep us ever mindful of this time of practice
   as a time of prayer and worship.
Each time music rises from our hearts
   it gives glory to You, our Lord and God.

May we practice holiness and kindness
   with the same devotion that we practice our music.
May each of our lives be a song of praise to You.

We ask this in the name of our Lord, Jesus Christ.

Amen +

PRAYER BEFORE A CHOIR PRACTICE

Before we begin our practice, let us pause for prayer:

silent prayer

Lord of Hosts,
  assist us as we practice
  in preparation for the Sacred Liturgy.
The blending of our different voices
  requires the attention of our hearts and minds.
May this concentration harmonize
  with a prayerful spirit within us
  as we prepare for our communal worship.

May each note we sing be a prayer,
  and may we be ever mindful
  of the sacredness of this special place.
May the attitude of our hearts,
  in our joyfulness as well as our difficulties,
  blend with the mood
  of this holy place of prayer.

Be with us, Lord, as we now begin
  in the name of the Father, Son, and Holy Spirit.

Amen +

PRAYER AFTER A CHOIR PRACTICE

Lord,
    before we depart, we thank You
    for the gift of our voices,
    for those who wrote the music we have practiced
    and for the gift of being able to serve—
    both our parish-community and You—
    with our music and song.

We pray that this time of practice
    has truly been a living prayer to You.

We ask Your Blessing as we depart,
    through Your Son, our Lord Jesus Christ.

Amen✝

PRAYER BEFORE PREPARING A HOMILY

Holy Jesus, Model of Preachers,
   You who delighted those who heard You
   with Your simple stories and profound insights,
   come to my aid as I prepare to create this homily.
My personal gifts for such a work seem limited,
   but I believe profoundly
   that if I but empty my heart of my self
   that You will flood that heart
   with words that You want spoken.

May the Sacred Words of Scripture
   fall like seeds upon my spirit
   to be nourished by the flesh and blood
   of my own sufferings and struggles to be holy.
Help me, Lord, to speak only what I believe,
   and to will to live what I shall proclaim
   so that my whole life may be my homily.

May I experience this time of preparation as prayer.
May my efforts to re-shape the message of the gospels—
   to fit this age and to touch those persons
   who seek You in the midst of their daily lives—
   be truly prayerful.

Send forth Your Spirit and touch my heart
   as I now begin this prayer
   in the name of the Father,
   and of the Son, and of the Holy Spirit.

Amen✝

THE PRAYER OF THE MEETING

As the number of ministries of the servants of God increases, so will the need to co-ordinate and direct these numerous manifestations of the Spirit. The meeting, the coming together to meet that need, is an important function in the life of the modern servant of God. Such a coming together should not only begin with a prayer; it should in fact be prayer. If this more and more common experience of us who serve is to become part of our spiritual transformation, we will need a new level of consciousness about what should happen at the meeting and how it should happen.

A meeting is a coming together and is therefore a communion. We should, by prayer and by our very attitude, keep this as the primary function before us. Indeed, every meeting has its business and administrative needs, but these should not cloud the communal sense of servants gathering in and for the Lord. A meeting is a gathering of hearts, spirits and dreams and consequently demands great respect and reverence for these sacred realities. We must be keenly conscious of how easily personal feelings can be injured in the common effort to find satisfying solutions during the work of our meetings, and we must be open, both before and after a meeting, to a prayerful reconciliation between persons. If our meetings are to be meetings of hearts centered in God, we will need to be aware of the Presence of the Divine Mystery even in the midst of disputes and disagreements. In this awareness, every meeting can become a lesson in humility, charity, and the mystery of how God is working in the midst of our lives.

Meetings, like meals, can often begin with a prayer but continue without prayerfulness. The sense of worship can easily become lost in the activity of the event. As we deal with the practical aspects of the agenda of a meeting, we must guard that we remain awake to the Presence of the Lord of Light at the heart of our gathering. To sustain this mindfulness, we might, for example, burn a candle or vigil light in the center of the meeting table as a visible and sacramental reminder that our meeting is more than an administrative function—a reminder that it is prayer and worship (see prayers on pages 120-121). For in meetings as in meals, we are to find delight in the Presence of the Divine Mystery in some of the most unlikely places: in potatoes or in programs, in agendas as well as in apples.

May the prayers in this section be an aid to all those who wish to make meetings a prayerful part of their service to God and the people of God.

PRAYERS
BEFORE MEETINGS

PRAYER BEFORE
A PARISH COUNCIL MEETING

Lord, God of Unity and Strength,
    we approach this meeting as a time of communion
    with You and with each other.
May the spirit of prayer not only begin our work
    but sustain it and conclude it as well.

The problems we must discuss are many
    and the solutions will not be easy,
    but may the final minutes of this meeting reveal
    that at all times
    we were reverent toward one another,
    and respectful of each other's ideas and positions.
May we, Lord, in this meeting
    seek not merely that we think alike
    but that we be united in heart and in purpose.
Although ideas and visions may divide,
    may our love for You and for each other unite us.

We pause now, in silence,
    so that each of us may invite You
    to be Companion and Consultor
    at this parish council meeting:

silent prayer

May we begin in Your Holy Name:
    Father, Son, and Holy Spirit.

Amen +

PRAYER BEFORE
A PARISH COUNCIL MEETING

Lord, our God,
    we ask Your Divine Assistance in the difficult task
    of representing the wishes of others.
Because we serve You
    in this service to the members of our parish,
    may this meeting serve to be
    a prayerful and worshipful gathering.

May our vision as leaders of our parish
    extend beyond material things
    and encompass the ideals of the gospel
    and of Your Son, Jesus Christ.
Help us to think beyond the boundaries of our parish
    and to be truly catholic—universal—
    in our service to the local and the global Church.
May we, by this meeting,
    hasten the coming of the Kingdom.

We begin in the name of the Father,
    and of the Son, and of the Holy Spirit.

Amen +

PRAYER BEFORE
A PARISH COUNCIL MEETING

God of Abraham, Isaac and Jacob,
    You have called us
    to be the servants of Your servants—
    our brothers and sisters in the parish.
We meet here as their representatives,
    and so we ask for the Grace of Your Guidance.
Help us to truly represent them
    and not simply ourselves.
May the true needs of our parish
    and the common good of all be our concern.
And above all, may Your Will in these matters
    become our Will.

Help us who serve in this elected position
    to remember that all of our concerns are aimed at
    the spiritual transformation of our parish-community.
May the material aspects we shall discuss
    not blind us to the primary work of our parish:
    the holiness of all its members.

May the Holy Spirit,
    who inspired the Pentecost meeting of the apostles,
    visit us and grant us the light of Divine Wisdom.
We ask this through our Lord, Jesus Christ,
    who lives with You and the Holy Spirit,
    forever and ever.

Amen +

PRAYER BEFORE
A PARISH COUNCIL MEETING

Holy Jesus, our Friend and Stronghold,
　　You who visited the apostles
　　as they labored with their fishing
　　and granted them success,
　　come and visit us in this meeting
　　so that the work of this session
　　may also be fruitful.

Untangle all the knots,
　　and smooth out the rough ways,
　　as we, with confidence,
　　begin this spiritual work of service
　　in the sign of Your Cross:
　　in the name of the Father,
　　and of the Son, and of the Holy Spirit.

Amen +

PRAYER BEFORE
A PARISH COUNCIL MEETING

Let us pause in silence
to be mindful of the Presence of our Lord and God
as we gather for this meeting:

silent prayer

Let us be mindful of the Divine Presence,
alive within each of us who is present.
Let us be aware of the Presence of the Divine Mystery
in the issues that we shall discuss,
in the concerns that are the work of our council:

silent prayer

Lord, with such mindfulness,
we now begin this parish council meeting.
Help us to sustain that consciousness throughout.
May we be respectful of the opinions of all:
reverential to the ideas of others
and to the manner in which they are presented.
As we represent the members of our parish-community,
may we also, at this meeting,
represent the love and understanding of our Lord
to each other.

May the Kingdom arrive sooner
because of the prayerfulness
of this parish council meeting.

Amen +

PRAYER BEFORE AN EDUCATIONAL MEETING

Lord, Divine Teacher,
   be with us as we begin this meeting.
Your Son's command to teach all nations
   is our concern.
Assist us so that this meeting
   will be for us who attend it
   an opportunity to learn as well.

In the process of dealing
   with the material issues at hand,
   may we learn how to treat each other's ideas
   with reverence and respect.
May we be instructed in the Divine Truth
   that in the variety of approaches—
   out of the rich differences among us—
   will come the balance of the Kingdom.
May we discover how to reject ideas
   without rejecting people
   and how to share visions
   though we do not share the same means
   for reaching our desired goals.

May this meeting, then, be for each of us
   a prayer, a lesson and an opportunity to be servants
   to those whom we represent.
We ask this through our Eternal Teacher and Master,
   Jesus Christ.

Amen +

PRAYER BEFORE A LITURGY MEETING

Lord of Holiness,
    we pause to be aware of Your Divine Presence,
    as we begin this time of planning.
Help us to harmonize
    the services and talents of each person here—
    not to draw attention to our own gifts—
    but so that we may assist the whole congregation,
    as well as each one of us,
    to lift up our hearts and minds to You in worship.

Reveal to us how we can blend
    a loving care of the ancient rituals
    with a continuous search for simple yet new ways
    to make our worship alive.

May we be true liturgists,
    seeking to enhance and fully participate in
    the Mystery of Your Holy Presence.
May prayer, worship and love
    be the primary motive of the work we shall now do.

We begin this prayerful task, with confidence,
    in the name of the Father, Son, and Holy Spirit.

Amen✚

PRAYER BEFORE A LITURGY MEETING

Eternal Lord and God,
    as ancient as the seasons
    are the rituals we shall plan.
Help us to be stewards of these sacred actions
    so that we may call into being
    a worship that is honest and holy.

Help us to rejoice
    in that which is always the same and unchanging,
    while finding delight in freshness and change.

May the needs of those who will pray this liturgy
    and the reverence we owe to You, our God,
    now guide this holy work
    which we begin in the sign of Your Holy Name:
    Father, Son, and Holy Spirit.

Amen +

PRAYER BEFORE ANY MEETING

Lord, Eternal God,
    we are about to begin our meeting,
    and we do so with the awareness
    that without Your Divine Presence
    here at the center of our meeting—
    and also within ourselves—
    our work will be empty.

Grace us with Your Wisdom and Vision;
    gift us with Holy Humor and Humility
    so that not only this meeting
    but all our lives
    may be a meeting place
    for Your Kingdom.

We ask this through our Lord, Jesus Christ,
    who lives with You
    in the unity of the Holy Spirit,
    now and forever.

Amen +

PRAYER BEFORE ANY MEETING

Lord, we rejoice in this opportunity
  to gather in Your Name.
Each time we come together,
  we can be gifted with Your Presence
  as we also meet the practical matters at hand.

We ask that the work of this meeting
  be a vessel for us to serve one another and You.
May the ritual of the agenda
  be a cause for communion among us.
Guide us who serve through this meeting
  so that our prejudgements and our personal histories
  do not hinder the purpose of this meeting
  or the coming of the Kingdom.

We ask this through Your Son, our Lord, Jesus,
  who lives with You and the Holy Spirit,
  now and forever.

Amen +

PRAYER BEFORE ANY MEETING

Lord, Source of All Our Strength,
    support each of us
    in this meeting that is now beginning.
Grant us the courage to be open to each other
    and to not be fearful of the new and different.
Strengthen us with a willingness to risk
    for the sake of Your Kingdom.

It is our wish, Lord and God,
    that the true business of this meeting
    be our spiritual transformation
    and not simply the accomplishment
    of tasks and projects.

We ask this of You as we now begin,
    in the name of the Father, Son, and Holy Spirit.

Amen +

PRAYER AT A TIME OF STALEMATE

CHAIRPERSON: Since we have reached an impasse,
   may I suggest that we stop for prayer:

Lord God, hear us as we pray;
   we have come to a position
   from which we are unable to move ahead in unison.
And so, we pause to ask Your Divine Assistance.
Let us back away from this issue
   so that we might view it from a vantage point
   not weighted down by personal interests
   or colored with a merely practical logic.
As we pray in silence, guide us to resolve this issue
   by the light of the gospels,
   with the Gentleness and Compassion of Christ
   and with true humility of heart:

silent prayer *(for perhaps five minutes—allowing*
   people to leave the table or meeting room for a
   silent period of reflection)

upon returning:

Lord, we come together again in Your Holy Name.
Having been nourished by stillness,
   and having heard the Divine Voice within our hearts,
   let us resume our meeting
   to see if we can reach a decision
   that is for our common good
   and for the good of the whole Church.

Amen +

PRAYERS
AFTER MEETINGS

PRAYER AFTER A LITURGY MEETING

Divine Lord of Power and Grace,
    we ask that You bless our work now completed
    and that our departure may be a prayerful one.
We pray that You would take our worshipful plans
    and place upon them the seal of Your Peace,
    so that they and we
    may give You glory and honor.

Show to us how to live lives
    that harmonize with the Sacred Liturgy,
    how to work in ways that are worship-filled
    and how, by the Grace of Your Son, Jesus,
    to pray always.

May all that we say and do,
    as well as the very attitude of our hearts,
    proclaim a liturgy of praise to You, our God.

Amen ✝

PRAYER AFTER ANY MEETING

Our Blessed Lord,
  You whose Power and Name
  we invoked at the beginning of this meeting,
  hear us now
  as we prayerfully conclude our gathering.

If any of us here
  by word or neglect has offended another,
  let him or her be sorry
  and seek a union of hearts before we finally depart.
For any misunderstanding or confusion
  for which any of us may have been responsible,
  let him or her be sorry, as we pause in silent prayer,
  so that we may depart in peace and communion:

silent prayer

Lord, we thank You for the honor of serving others
  by our presence here at this meeting.
May our service as well as our time and effort
  be a prayer of praise to You, our Lord and God.

May the Blessing and Protection of God be upon us:
  in the name of the Father,
  and of the Son, and of the Holy Spirit.

Amen ✝

PRAYER AFTER ANY MEETING

Lord of Day and Night,
of beginnings and endings,
as we prepare to conclude this meeting,
we once again lift up our hearts to You,
the Divine Source of All Life.

We thank You for the gifts that have been present
within this act of service to the community.
For the gifts of fellowship and understanding,
of mutual respect and shared vision,
we are grateful.
For the gifts of perseverance
and of insight into the common concerns we share,
for these and all other graces, we are thankful.

As You have blessed our coming together,
now bless our departure and journeys homeward.
May Your Ever-Youthful Blessing
be upon us,
in the name of the Father, Son, and Holy Spirit.

Amen +

PRAYER AFTER ANY MEETING

Before we adjourn this meeting,
   let us pause for silent prayer
   in gratitude to our Lord for the Divine Presence
   at the center of our gathering:

silent prayer

We lift up into Your Divine Heart
   the material concerns that we have discussed.
With Your Holy Assistance,
   may we carry forward the work we have agreed upon.

Remember the needs of our parish-community,
   especially that we may, all of us, grow daily
   in the image of Your Son, our Lord, Jesus Christ.

May You accompany us homeward
   and bless our departure with Your Abiding Presence.

Amen ✝

PRAYER AFTER ANY MEETING

Lord, it is never easy to balance
    all our mutual ideas and visions.
And so we are grateful
    for Your Sacred Presence at this meeting now ended.
For the compass-guidance of the gospel
    which holds up for us
    the clear ideal of self-sacrificing service,
    we thank You.

If, in the course of our discussion
    of material and practical concerns,
    divisions among us have been created,
    we ask that You mend them now
    by the Healing Grace of Your Son, our Lord.

We pause now in silent prayer
    to lift up into Your Divine Heart
    the following project (concern)
    which we have agreed upon in this meeting:

silent prayer

Unless You bless this work, it will not prosper;
    if You will its success, we cannot fail.
May Your Blessing be upon it
    and upon each of us as well.
May You surround our parish-community
    with the Rainbow of Your Peace.

We ask this in the name of our Lord, Jesus Christ.

Amen +

PRAYER AFTER A LONG MEETING

Lord, our God,
 this has been a long meeting,
 and we are now tired.
But like the apostles
 after a long night fishing,
 we need Your Blessing to confirm our efforts.

Touch with Your Power all that we have decided.
May the numerous concerns of this meeting
 advance the Kingdom,
 build up the Body of Christ, the Church,
 and give glory to You.

May You bless each of us in Your Holy Name:
 Father, Son, and Holy Spirit.

Amen +

PRAYER BEFORE A MEETING
USING A SACRAMENTAL

A candle at the center of the meeting table is lit as the prayer begins.

Radiant Lord,
    may this candle which we now light
    be a sacrament of Your Presence
    here among us at this meeting.

As the light streams forth from this candle,
    may Your Divine Wisdom flow
    into every detail of our meeting.
By the light of Your Divine Presence,
    may we truly see You, our God,
    in one another,
    in all the issues that we face
    and even in the midst of our differences of opinion.

In Your Holy Will,
    may all things work together for good,
    may all that we shall discuss be blessed
    and hasten the building up of Your Kingdom
    here in our parish.

We ask this through Christ, our Lord.

Amen +

PRAYER AFTER A MEETING
USING A SACRAMENTAL

Lord, the work of this session is now complete.
As we prepare to extinguish this candle,
    may its light live on in each of us.
May our hearts be inflamed with Your Love.

May that light which we take into our hearts
    remove anything of word or thought
    that may have caused pain or injury
    in the course of this meeting.

Through our mutual sacrifice and prayer,
    may Your Divine Light shine even brighter
    within this our parish-community
    and within each of our homes.

May Your Blessing grant to each of us
    a safe return to our homes and personal lives:
    in the name of the Father, Son, and Holy Spirit.

Amen✝

The candle is extinguished

SACRED DRESS FOR THE SERVANTS OF GOD

Those who serve directly at the altar may wear special vestments as signs of their office. However, all who serve share in Christ's priesthood, and thus all who serve, should be vested for their service—but with a very special vestment. As the psalmist prays: "Your priests shall be clothed in holiness" (Ps. 131:9 *The Psalms: Singing Version*). And so, each time we come to serve—in whatever function, role or activity—we should be accordingly robed in holiness.

Sacred service by its demands for perfection—excellence both at the altar and away from it—should slowly but progressively vest each of us in that most sacred of vestments. That divine activity of clothing us in holiness is in truth at the heart of service to God. In fact, ministry is not intended to gratify those who serve but rather to purify them—and to purify them even in the midst of the difficulties of daily life. The call to holiness is a call to see in the sacrifices and pains of life that the Divine Mystery is at work cleansing us for even more perfect service.

No one comes within the sacred circle of the altar completely pure in motive or intention. But as we surrender more fully to the mysterious will of God, we will find that our motives are made more and more pure and that our service is made more whole and holy. However, if we should approach the time of sacred service with anything in our hearts that is not at peace with all, with anything in our lives that does not mirror the Mystery whom we serve, then we must take time to allow ourselves to be touched by the grace and compassion of God. In prayer we must lay open our troubled hearts and our less than perfect lives and allow God to properly vest us for our service.

May these prayers of devotion be a daily aid to our becoming more fully clothed in Christ, to our being vested in holiness.

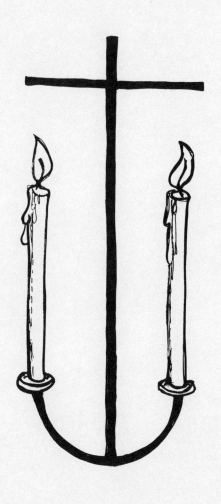

PRAYERS OF DEVOTION
FOR THE SERVANTS OF GOD

PRAYER OF PREPARATION
FOR ONE WHO SERVES

Lord, my God,
    it is almost time for me to begin my service.
Help me, I pray, to perform my appointed task
    with dignity but also with great humility.

I realize that You may choose anyone or anything
    to be Your vessel of grace.
I am humbled by Your choice of me
    and strive to be worthy of my ministry.
I also realize that pride prevents the flow
    of Your Divine Grace;
        so, while I fully appreciate the dignity of my work,
        I guard against being prideful or arrogant.

With Your Gracious Assistance,
    my daily work and life will support and ennoble
    my service to the Church and to the Kingdom.
May my whole life be a reflection
    of that service to the parish and to the Church.
May this holy work I am about to perform
    call forth from within me
    greater and greater personal holiness.

May Your Blessing be upon me
    in the name of the Father,
    and of the Son, and of the Holy Spirit.

Amen +

PRAYER FOR DIVINE ASSISTANCE

My Lord, I feel a bit nervous and fearful
    as I prepare for my sacred function.
Help me to realize that even in my mistakes
    You will be given glory and praise.
Free me of unnecessary anxiety, of excessive concern,
    so that I may fully realize
    that I am but a channel of Your Grace.

I take courage in the truth
    that once called to serve You, my God,
    and the needs of Your people,
    I will be given the necessary graces
    to perform the work that is mine.
Let my heart be anchored in You,
    as I take refuge in You, my Rock and my Stronghold.

I ask this through Jesus Christ, our Lord,
    who lives with You and the Holy Spirit,
    forever and ever.

Amen ✝

PRAYER FOR PROTECTION
FROM ROUTINE-LIKE RITUAL
IN THE SACRED LITURGY

Lord, God of the Ever-New,
    before I enter into this sacred ritual,
    I ask Your Divine Assistance.
Protect me from the blindness of routine and repetition
    that causes ritual to become lifeless.
While the actions I shall perform are familiar to me,
    let them truly reveal, this day, Your Face.

Sacred is my service.
Renew within my heart a sense of reverence and awe
    for all that is included
    within the sacred circle of this Altar-Table.
Inspire me to celebrate and serve at this Liturgy
    as though it were the first time I had been honored
    to minister to You in this way
    and perhaps as if it were to be the last.
May I show a profound respect for all that is sacred,
    whether I am alone
    or in the presence of the entire community.

I ask this in the name of our Lord, Jesus Christ.

Amen +

PRAYER FOR PRAYERFULNESS

Hear me, Lord, as I make this request.
Be present to me so that this time of service
   will be my prayer to You.

While it will be necessary for me to attune my mind
   to the practical necessities of what is to happen,
   let my attention to detail be a prayer of worship.
Although I may not feel prayerful
   as I open the way for the worship of others,
   may my service itself be a sacrifice of devotion,
   for I know that You, my Lord and my God,
   are always present when even two or three
   come together in the name of Christ.

Remind me to prepare spiritually
   for each of these times of service.
By my personal prayer, I prepare my heart
   so that it will be in full communion with You,
   before, during and after this sacred encounter.

Amen✝

PRAYER OF GRATITUDE
AFTER A TIME OF SERVICE

Lord,
    my time of service is now ended,
    but before I return to my daily life,
    I ask Your Blessing.
Bless me, Lord, with a desire to serve others
    not only in an official capacity
    but whenever and wherever I meet those in need.
Remind me as I return home
    that I serve You best
    by seeking holiness in my personal life,
    holiness in my home and lifework.

Show to me that in Your Eyes
    all service is an act of love,
    a sign of devotion and dedication.
Reveal to me how all service is an act of faith,
    a testimonial to the truth that You, my Lord,
    are present in all whom I serve.
Finally, allow me to see
    that each act of service is an act of hope,
    that in humble but loving deeds of assistance,
    the Kingdom will come into our world.

Be patient, Lord, as I struggle to learn
    these ancient but ever-youthful truths.
I ask this in the name of the Father,
    and of the Son, and of the Holy Spirit.

Amen +

PRAYER OF GRATITUDE
AFTER A TIME OF SERVICE

Lord, I have only a few minutes,
    but I cannot leave without thanking You
    for the dignity and the grace of my ministry.
May I never be so busy as to forget to thank You
    for the great privilege that is mine in serving.

May my thanksgiving be expressed
    in the way I live out
    all that now follows my time of service.

Bless me, Lord, in Your Name:
    Father, Son, and Holy Spirit.

Amen ✝

PRAYER OF GRATITUDE
AFTER A TIME OF SERVICE

Beloved Lord,
   I thank You for this time of service just ended.
While my duties have been simple,
   they remind me of my primal vocation:
   to be a servant and friend of Yours.

My prayerful period of ministry
   has once again awakened within me a desire
   to be more than an ordinary Christian.
May the prayerfulness of this moment
   be a frequent visitor in the hours and days ahead.
By my daily prayer and devotion,
   may I become more a whole and holy person.

I ask that each time I come to serve
   both You and the parish-community
   I will find food for my heart,
   strength for my spirit
   and confirmation in my dream to become
   the person that You have called me to be.

I ask this in Your Name:
   Father, Son, and Holy Spirit.

Amen +

PRAYER OF GRATITUDE
AFTER A TIME OF SERVICE

Eternal Lord,
    I desire to share in the conversation and communion
    of those who have gathered after this celebration.
But before I join in this fellowship,
    I seek the communion
    of Your Continuous Presence in my life.

I have felt Your Sacred Touch in this celebration
    and desire to respond to it
    with all my heart and with all my strength.
I seek to love You
    both in service and in prayer and devotion.

Bless those with whom I have served,
    bless those who have taken part in this celebration,
    and bless me, Your servant,
    with Your Great Grace and Peace.

Amen +

A GOSPEL ON THE SACRAMENT OF SERVICE

After he [Jesus] had washed their feet, he put his cloak back on and reclined at table once more. He said to them:

"Do you understand what I just did for you?
You address me as 'Teacher' and 'Lord,'
and fittingly enough,
for that is what I am.
But if I washed your feet—
I who am Teacher and Lord—
then you must wash each other's feet.
What I just did was to give you an example:
as I have done, so you must do.
I solemnly assure you,
no slave is greater than his master;
no messenger outranks the one who sent him.
Once you know all these things,
blest will you be if you put them into practice."

John 13:12-17

REFLECTION ON THE EXAMPLE OF JESUS

Eternal God,
   I struggle to put into practice in my own life
   the beautiful example of my Lord.
By my service to others,
   small and unimportant as it is,
   I strive to pattern my life upon that of Jesus.
To be Your servant is indeed to be
   a messenger who proclaims the secret of the gospels:
   that in humble and loving service,
   God becomes present in our midst.

While I strive daily to "know all these things,"
   I often find it difficult to "put them into practice."
Help me, Lord, by Your Grace
   not to seek positions of honor or authority
   but rather to pursue the path of humble service.
Regardless of the task or ministry
   that I am entrusted to perform,
   may I find in it the lesson of the Last Supper,
   when my Lord washed His friends' feet
   As an example of holy service for my life.

May the saintly servants of God, the ancient ones,
   together with Mary, the handmaid of the Lord,
   daily help me in my efforts,
   to be a humble servant of the people of God.

Amen +

A GOSPEL ON THE REWARD OF SERVANTS

[And Jesus said to His disciples,]
"If one of you had a servant plowing or herding
sheep and he came in from the fields, would you say
to him, 'Come and sit down at table'? Would you not
rather say, 'Prepare my supper. Put on your apron
and wait on me while I eat and drink. You can eat
and drink afterward'? Would he be grateful to the
servant who was only carrying out his orders? It is
quite the same with you who hear me. When you
have done all you have been commanded to do, say,
'We are useless servants. We have done no more
than our duty.' "

Luke 17:7-10

REFLECTION ON A SAYING OF JESUS

Lord, as I reflect upon the words of Your Son,
   I realize I must keep watch over my heart
   lest I seek public acclaim in my work for You.
Help me to seek to serve with single-mindedness
   and with purity of intention.
When I have finished my work, show to me
   that it has simply been my duty
   and not cause for gold awards or lavish praise.

By Holy Baptism
   I have been initiated as Your servant,
   as a servant of the Kingdom,
   and have become one with Christ
   who was to receive the cross and suffering
   in return for His ministry to others—
   though He was finally gifted by You
   with the Fullness of Life in His Resurrection.
May I, Your servant,
   seek to perform my tasks out of love and devotion,
   seeking not the fruits of my service
   but only You as my reward.

For my service, my Lord and God,
   gift me, Your servant, with Your Abounding Life,
   both now and in the life to come.

Amen +

MARY'S CANTICLE

"My being proclaims the greatness of the Lord,
   my spirit finds joy in God my savior,
For he has looked upon his servant in her lowliness;
   all ages to come shall call me blessed.
God who is mighty has done great things for me,
   holy is his name;
His mercy is from age to age
   on those who fear him.
He has shown might with his arm;
   he has confused the proud in their inmost thoughts.
He has deposed the mighty from their thrones
   and raised the lowly to high places.
The hungry he has given every good thing,
   while the rich he has sent empty away.
He has upheld Israel his servant,
   ever mindful of his mercy;
Even as he promised our fathers,
   promised Abraham and his descendants forever."

Luke 1:46-55

PSALMS FOR SERVANTS

Come, bless the LORD,
  all you servants of the LORD
Who stand in the house of the LORD
  during the hours of night.
Lift up your hands toward the sanctuary,
  and bless the LORD.
May the LORD bless you from Zion,
  the maker of heaven and earth.

(Psalm 134)

Praise the name of the LORD;
  Praise, you servants of the LORD
Who stand in the house of the LORD,
  in the courts of the house of our God.
Praise the LORD, for the LORD is good;
  sing praise to his name, which we love;
For the LORD has chosen Jacob for himself,
  Israel for his own possession.

(Psalm 135: 1-4)

How shall I make a return to the LORD
  for all the good he has done for me?
The cup of salvation I will take up,
  and I will call upon the name of the LORD;
My vows to the LORD I will pay
  in the presence of all his people.
Precious in the eyes of the LORD
  is the death of his faithful ones.
O LORD, I am your servant. . .

(Psalm 116:12-16)

RENEWAL OF DEDICATION TO SERVICE

Some who serve are ordained to that office of servant-hood; others are commissioned or installed, and all who serve may be blessed by the act of service itself. The occasion of a ritual or prayer that commemorates an individual act or a whole life of service has the power to raise our consciousness of the fact that it is God who has called us to this service. Aware of the continuous challenge of being servants of God, we have need of frequent, if not continuous, rededication to a life of service. A gesture of rededication at special times can serve to make us more conscious of the sacred trust that is ours through our service.

Such acts of dedication could well take place on the anniversary of ordination or commissioning or on the anniversary of receiving the Sacrament of Baptism, the primary sacred act of dedication to ministry. Another most fitting occasion is the feast of Holy Thursday when we commemorate our Lord's washing of His disciples' feet as a sign of the sacred trust of servanthood being passed on to them. Pentecost, the feast of singing the praises of the Holy Spirit, the source of countless gifts distributed among God's people—all for the building up of the Body of Christ—is still another feast day that invites a conscious act of love and gratitude.

Regardless of what day or days we choose, frequent renewal by times of prayer may be of great assistance to us in the search for sanctity. Such rituals, like the prayer-ritual that follows, are external signs intended to strengthen an invisible and internal reality. They reinforce our will to serve with love and humility and the desire to make that determination the continuous dedication of our hearts.

This concluding prayer seeks to sum up the spirituality of service that has unfolded through the prayer pages of this book. May it, as well as the whole of this manual for worship, serve as a source of nourishment and a vehicle of prayerful expression for all those who seek the royal path to holiness through their service.

DEDICATION FOR A SERVANT OF GOD

Lord God, You who know the hidden parts of my heart,
   come now and fill me with the spirit of sincerity
   as I dedicate myself to You
   and to service within Your Kingdom.
Lord, I desire to serve You and others
   with a totality of heart, soul and strength.
I strive to live within the simplicity of the gospels,
   open and obedient to Your Voice
   and chaste and whole in my loving.

Lord and Divine Friend,
   I dedicate myself anew to the vows of my Baptism,
   to a life of prayer and worship of You.
I re-commit myself to being a servant
   to the needs of those around me
   and to the needs of all the world.
May I find my holiness and salvation
   here, in this place and at this time,
   where You, my God, have placed me.

Lord, I marvel that You, in Your Divine Wisdom,
   have chosen me to be Your servant
   and Your instrument of creative salvation.
May my ministry, complete with failings and stumblings,
   be leaven for Your Kingdom to rise in our world.
Bless me now with Your Love,
   as I strive to be Your friend and holy servant.
May I live out this dedication and commitment
   in the name of the Father, Son, and Holy Spirit.

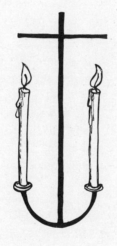